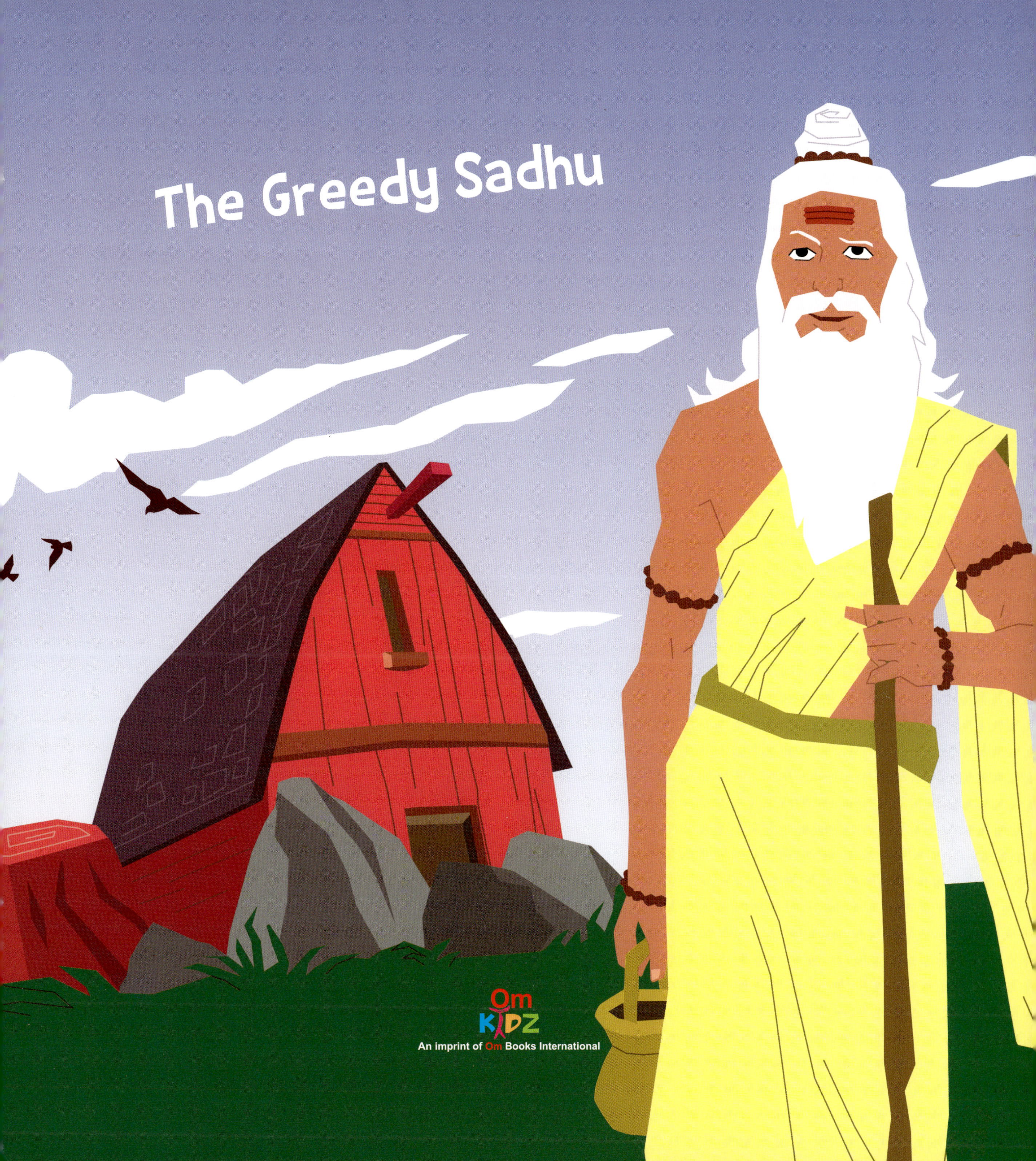
The Greedy Sadhu
Om KIDZ
An imprint of Om Books International

A sadhu lived in a hermitage in a forest. There was a small village near this forest. The sadhu was a cheat but had used his charms to win over the headman of the village. The headman treated the sadhu with respect and took care of all his needs. One day, the headman decided to hide the gold he owned in a safe place to protect it from dacoits.

"I shall bury the gold in the sadhu's hermitage!" he thought. "The dacoits won't attack a holy place."

The headman put all the gold he possessed into a pot and carried it to the sadhu's hermitage.

"I wish to hide all my gold in your hermitage to keep it safe from dacoits, O Holy One," the headman said to the sadhu.

The sadhu agreed. As the headman buried his pot of gold, the sadhu pretended to meditate, but saw from the corner of his eyes the spot where the headman had buried the gold.

Then the headman left the hermitage. A couple of days later, the greedy sadhu dug up the earth to remove the pot of gold. He buried it in the hermitage but in a different spot. Then, he visited the headman.

"I have decided to leave this place," the sadhu declared.

"But why, O Holy One?" the headman exclaimed. "Haven't I taken good care of you? Are you offended?" he asked.

"No!" the sadhu replied. "That is not the reason I wish to leave. You see, we sadhus have renounced the world and abandoned the pleasures of life. Hence, we cannot stay attached to any place for a long time. So, I must say goodbye to you!"

The village headman was sad to bid farewell to the sadhu. As the sadhu travelled out of the village, a sudden thought struck him.

"What if the headman suspects me of stealing his gold?"

He quickly pulled out a straw from a hut in the village and put it in his hair. Then he returned to the house of the headman who was seated with his good friend, a merchant from the village.

"Welcome back!" the headman greeted the sadhu happily. "Have you changed your mind and returned O Holy One?" he asked.

"No!" the sadhu replied. "I came to return something. We sadhus do not take anything that does not belong to us. Here is the straw from the roof of your house that got stuck on my head as I was leaving."

The sadhu handed the straw to the headman and took his leave.

"He is truly a noble man. Why, he won't even take a straw that doesn't belong to him!" the headman marvelled. But the merchant smelled a rat!

"Have you given him anything valuable for safe-keeping?" the merchant enquired. The headman mentioned the pot of gold he had buried in the sadhu's hermitage.

"Let us go and see if it's still there," the merchant said. The two friends rushed to the hermitage only to discover that the pot of gold was missing.

"He couldn't have travelled far," the merchant urged. "Let us catch the thief!"

The two ran ahead and managed to catch the sadhu.

"Where is the headman's gold?" the merchant demanded.

"Are you accusing a sadhu who has renounced the world?" the sadhu asked.

"Tell us where the gold is or you will have to renounce your life!" the merchant threatened the sadhu.

"Please don't hurt me!" the sadhu exclaimed. I shall tell you where the pot of gold is buried."

He led the headman and the merchant to the spot where he had buried the gold.

"Leave this village immediately," the headman ordered the sadhu. "Do not set foot here again!"

The greedy sadhu fled the village and was never seen again.

The Mosquito And The Carpenter

In the city of Benares, there once lived a carpenter who struggled to make ends meet. He had three grown-up sons as well and needed to work hard to support his family. One day, the carpenter was busy working in his yard as he studied the wood and the planks that he had collected. He wanted to build something new and was getting ready to begin work. The carpenter was not a young man. His hair had already turned grey, and he had a bald patch. As he thought harder, a mosquito landed right on top of his head.

"Ouch!" the carpenter exclaimed as the mosquito delivered a sharp sting on his bald patch. "Bzzz!" the mosquito danced around the carpenter's head as he tried his best to chase it away. No matter what he did, the mosquito kept returning and stinging him.

The carpenter turned to one of his sons who was seated next to him and requested, "Son, there is a mosquito that is biting me. It has settled right on top of my head. Please drive it away before it stings me again!"

"Do not move, dear father," the son requested. "I shall get rid of the mosquito and ease your pain with one quick blow!" he declared. "Wait for me! I shall be right back," the son said and ran into the house.

A holy man who was passing by observed this exchange between father and son. He stopped to

watch what would happen next as his curiosity had been aroused by the conversation between the two. Minutes later, the carpenter's son returned, carrying an axe. The holy man's jaw dropped in surprise.

"Oh! This mosquito will be the death of me," the carpenter exclaimed. "It keeps stinging me again and again. Get rid of the pest now," he ordered his son who stood behind him with his axe.

"Your wish is my command, father," the son stated as he raised his axe and brought it down on his father's head in a mighty blow. The holy man watched in horror as the carpenter's head split into two. The old carpenter died and the mosquito flew away.

"Oh no!" the son exclaimed. "I missed the mosquito and hit my father, instead!"

"It is better to have an enemy who possesses common sense than have a son who is senseless," the holy man stated to himself. "Fear of revenge will surely stop a man from killing his enemy but a son lacking sense will easily kill a father just like the carpenter's son has killed his own father!"

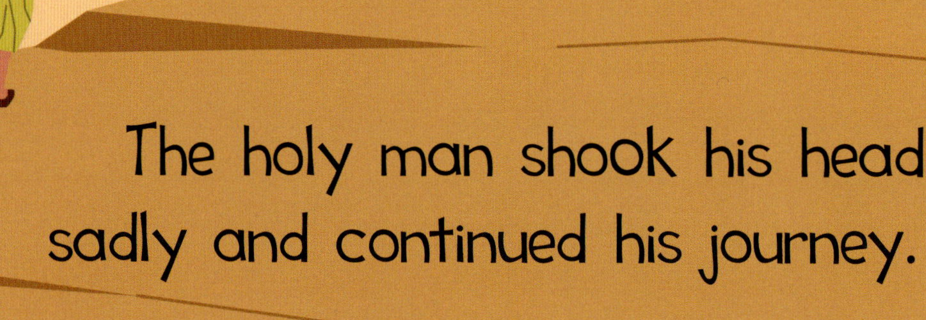

The holy man shook his head sadly and continued his journey.

Later, the unfortunate carpenter's last rites were conducted by his family on the banks of the holy river Ganga. His son wept over the loss of his father.

The Baby Quail Who Could Not Fly Away
Om KIDZ
An imprint of Om Books International

Once upon a time, there lived a baby quail. He had small feet and wings but could not walk or fly just yet. His parents brought back food for him to their nest and fed him lovingly from their beaks.

Forest fires were common where these birds nested. One day, there was a forest fire. At the first signs of smoke, all the birds began flying away from their nests.

"Save yourselves while you can," the other birds urged the parents of the baby quail as they left their nests. But the baby quail's parents refused to

abandon him even as the fire approached the tree in which they had their nest. But as the fire reached the nest, they were forced to flee to save their lives.

The little baby quail, left alone in the nest, watched all the trees catch fire and burn. He also observed that the forest fire had destroyed everything that lay in its path and was out of control now.

"I can do nothing to save myself now as I can't fly away like the other birds," the baby quail thought helplessly. Then he thought about his parents.

"My parents loved me so much. They built a nest for me and always fed me before they ate themselves. They stayed with me till the very last moment and did not fly away earlier like the other birds. They only flew away when they realised that

I could not be saved and they would die too if they stayed back," thought the baby quail.

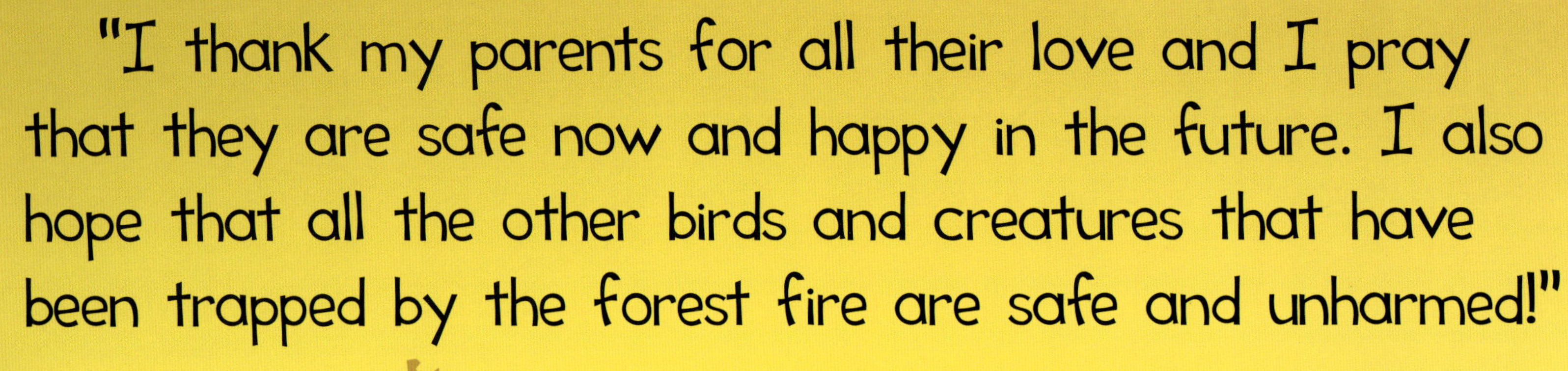

"I thank my parents for all their love and I pray that they are safe now and happy in the future. I also hope that all the other birds and creatures that have been trapped by the forest fire are safe and unharmed!"

The baby quail prayed for everyone's safety. "I am all alone here, now, and although I have feet, I cannot run away. Even though I have wings, I'm not capable of flying to safety. But I can still think.

"I have a mind that is pure and that functions unlike my wings and my feet. My mind tells me that I haven't harmed anyone. So, I have nothing to fear. It also tells me that I have an innocent truthfulness within me."

Then, a great miracle took place. The innocent truthfulness within the baby quail grew and kept growing till it was larger than the baby quail himself.

God noticed the innocent truthfulness of the baby quail and was moved. God made sure that the new-born truthfulness of the baby quail was merged with the ancient purity of wholesomeness and the Power of Truth.

"May the baby quail who could not fly away and all the birds and other beings that are trapped by the forest fire be saved immediately!" God declared. "Let this forest be safe from such forest fires for a period of a million years!"

And so it came to be!

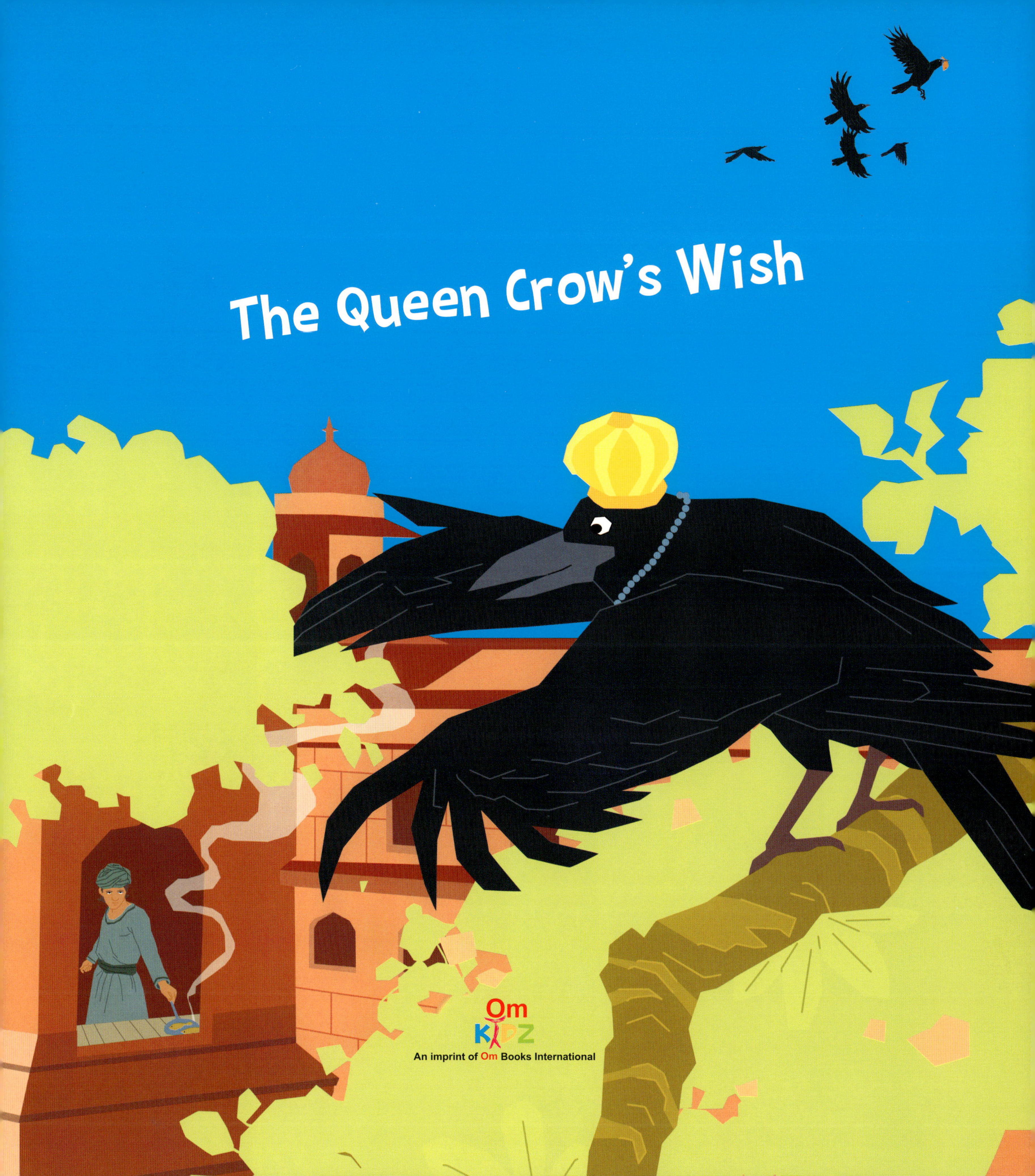
The Queen Crow's Wish
Om
KIDZ
An imprint of Om Books International

In the holy city of Benaras, there lived an army of crows. The king of the crows loved his queen dearly and was prepared to do anything for her. One day, the king and the queen flew past the palace kitchen of Benaras, where the cook was busy preparing food. Entranced by the smell emerging from the kitchen window, the curious queen crow peeked into the kitchen.

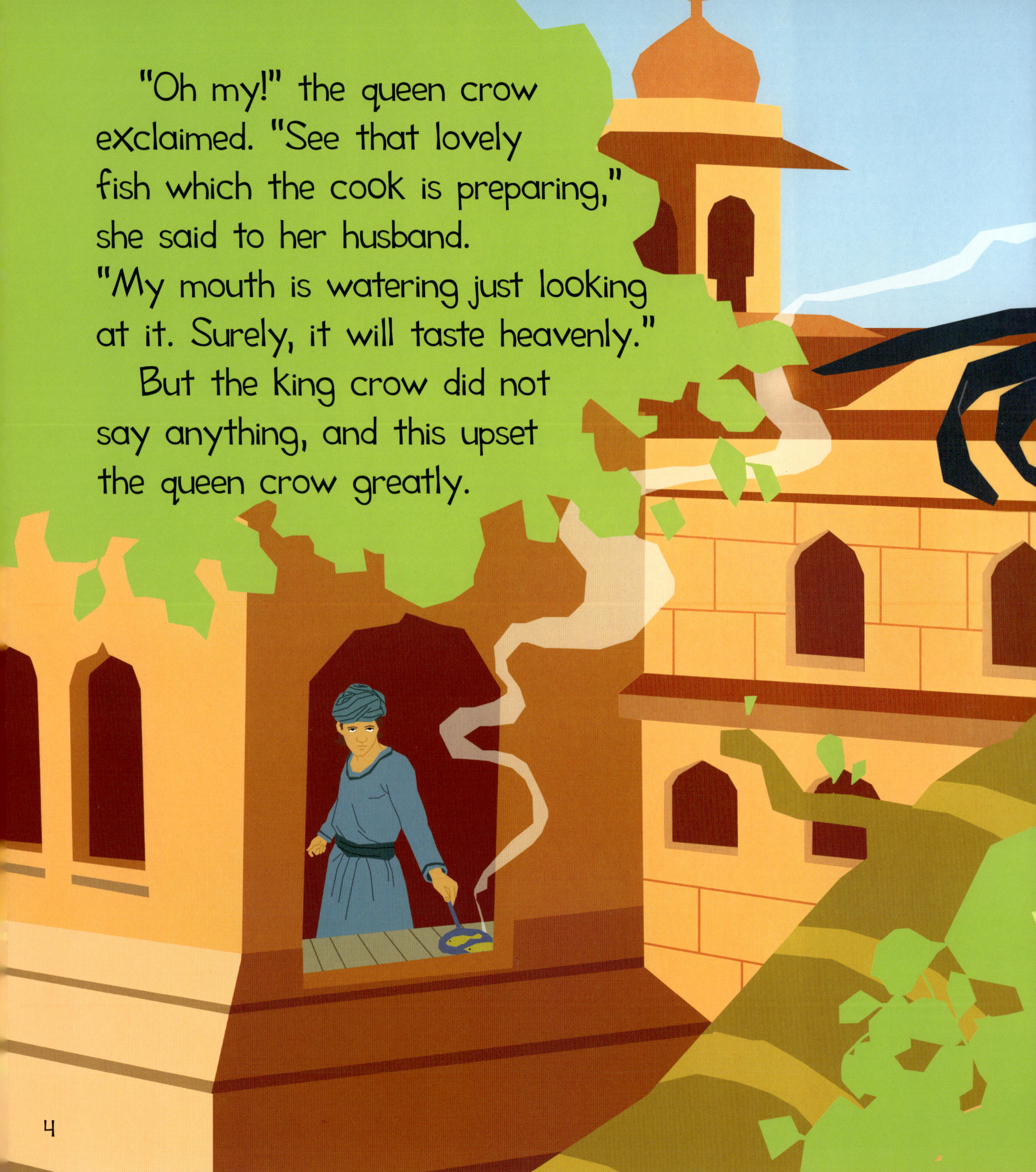

"Oh my!" the queen crow exclaimed. "See that lovely fish which the cook is preparing," she said to her husband. "My mouth is watering just looking at it. Surely, it will taste heavenly."

But the king crow did not say anything, and this upset the queen crow greatly.

"Let us go and look for some food, my dear," the king crow suggested, but his queen sulked and refused to go out.

"I do not want to eat the same food every day," the queen crow stated.

"What do you want, my dear?" the king crow asked in surprise.

"Get me the fish cooked by the royal cook in the palace. I shall only have that and nothing else," the queen crow stated firmly.

"But, my dear..." the king crow protested, but was interrupted by the queen crow.

"I shall eat that fish or I shall fast unto death," the queen crow said stubbornly.

A worried king crow sat on the tree for a while, and decided to send for his general. He then explained the problem to his general.

"The queen wishes to eat the fish cooked in the royal kitchen," the king crow explained.

"The queen shall have her wish granted, Your Highness!" the general replied. "I shall try my best!"

The general of the crows gathered eight of his bravest soldiers.

"My brave crows!" he addressed them. "We have to leave on a mission."

Led by the general, the crows flew off and landed on the roof of the palace kitchen where the general explained his plan to them, "When the cook takes the food from the kitchen to serve to the king,

I shall attack him and make him drop the dishes on the floor. Four of you must carry away the fish in your beaks and four of you must take the rice. Make sure you fill your beaks with the rice and fish so that our queen can eat to her heart's content!" the general of the crows ordered.

The general of the crows waited patiently till the moment was right. As the cook left the kitchen to reach the courtyard of the palace, the general flew in to attack him.

"Oh my god!" the cook exclaimed as he dropped the dishes in fright. The eight crows immediately flew in, stuffed their beaks with rice and fish, and flew away.

The king of Benaras had watched everything from his balcony.

"Catch that wicked crow that attacked my cook!" he ordered and soon the general of the crows was captured.

"I have succeeded in my mission!" the general of the crows thought happily as he was presented before the king of Benaras. "Let them do whatever they want with me, now."

"You have risked your life and stolen my food!" the king accused the crow. "Why?" he demanded.

"I have only done my duty," the general of the crows explained. "My queen wanted to eat the fish and rice that had been prepared for Your Majesty and I had promised my King that I would go to any length to get my queen the food!"

The King of Benaras was impressed by the loyalty displayed by the general of the crows.

"This crow is willing to lay down his life for his king!" he thought in admiration. "Instead of being punished, he should be rewarded!"

The king ordered that the general of the crows be set free and also declared that a portion of his food be sent every day to the king and the queen of the crows. The king also ordered that rice should be cooked for all the crows in the palace kitchen. The general of the crows flew away happily!

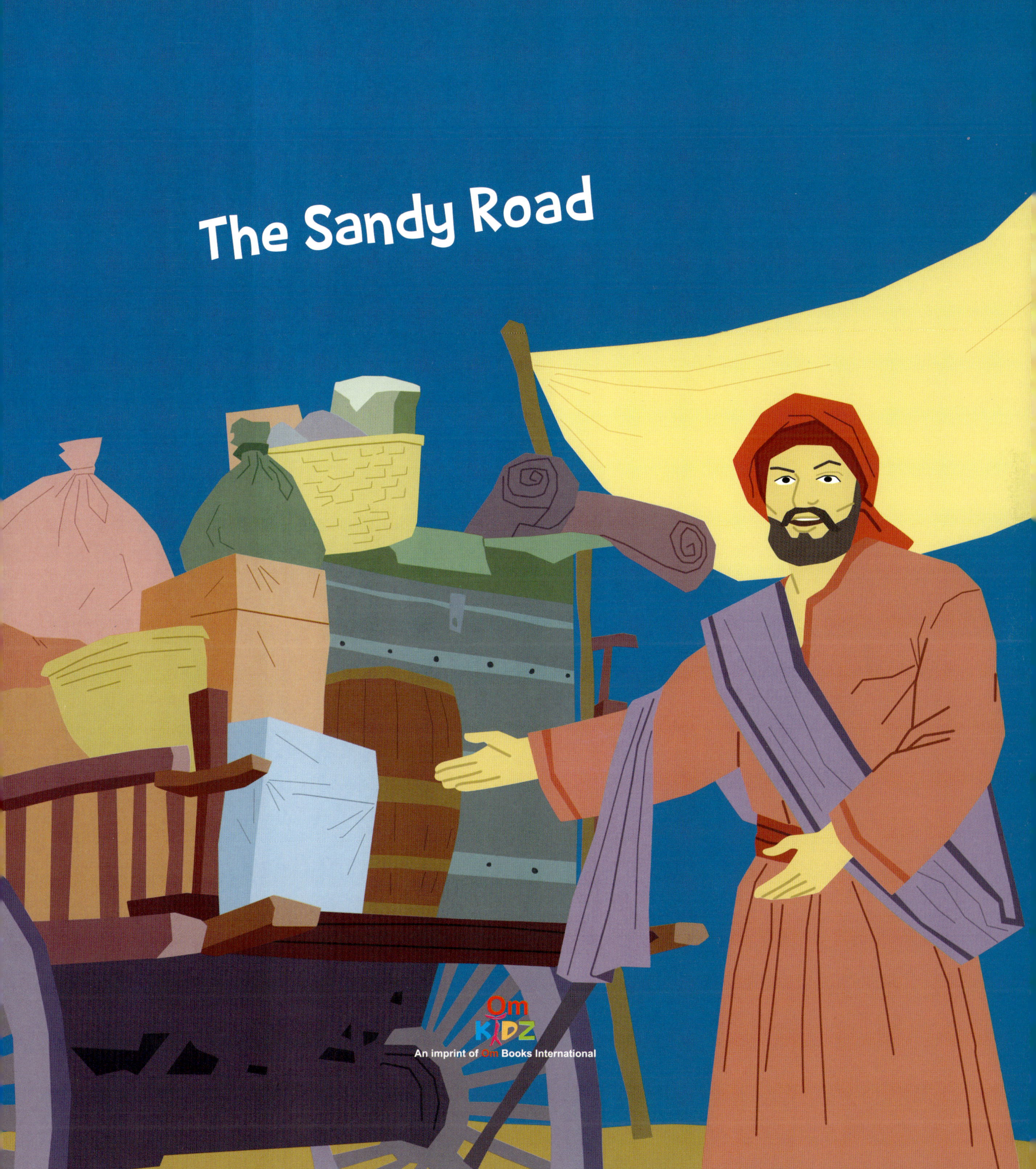
The Sandy Road
Om
KIDZ
An imprint of Om Books International

A merchant from a small village decided to sell his goods in town to make more profit. Accompanied by his men and a guide, he set off one day. Apart from the goods, they also carried water, rice and firewood as they had to cross a desert. When the merchant and his men reached the desert, the hot sand made it impossible for them to continue walking.

"We shall travel in the night when the sand is cooler," the merchant said to his men, "Let us rest during the day!"

One of the merchant's men knew how to read the position of the stars and guided them across the desert at night. The merchant and his men travelled all night. They stopped only at dawn to relax and set up their camp. The oxen were removed from the carts and fed. A fire was made, rice was cooked, and all the men ate before going to sleep. A huge covering was laid over the carts and the oxen to protect them from the hot sun, and the men rested till sunset.

At sunset, the men built a fire, cooked again and ate a hearty meal. Then, the covering was folded up and loaded onto the carts along with the supplies. The oxen were tied to the carts and the men resumed their journey.

The merchant and his men travelled for many nights, resting all day in the desert. Only the guide couldn't take rest even during the day. Soon they would reach their destination. All the men were very happy because their journey across the desert had exhausted them.

"Throw away the water and the firewood to lighten the heavy load. We shall reach the town tomorrow," the merchant ordered after they had finished their evening meal and were about to set off.

The guide was very tired as he had not slept during the day unlike the others. Eventually, he dozed off in the cart, instead of guiding the oxen. The oxen kept travelling through the night and the guide awoke only at daybreak.

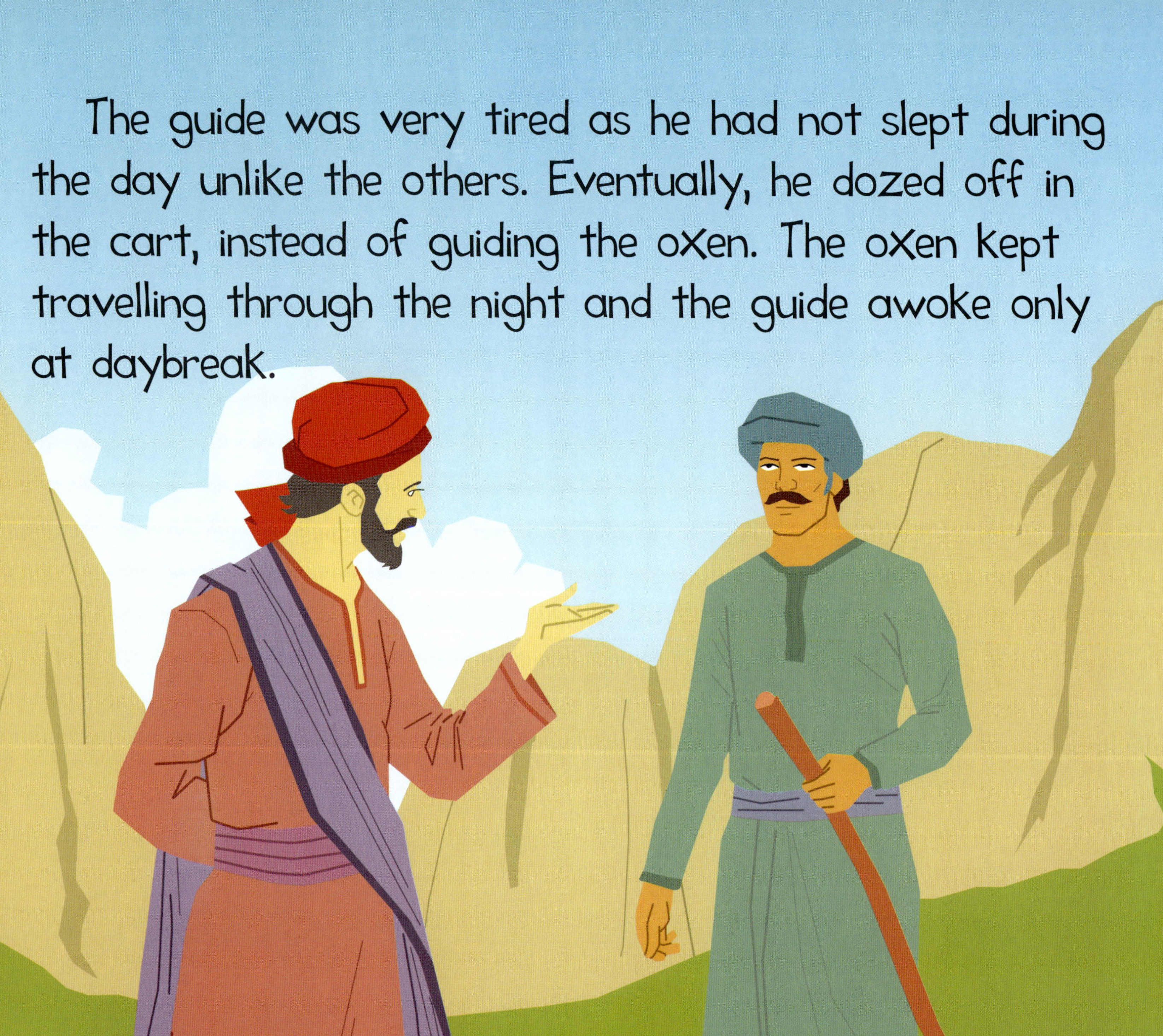

"Halt!" the guide commanded the cart drivers. "We have returned to the same place where we were last night," he declared. "I had fallen asleep and did not notice that the oxen had turned around!"

The men and the oxen were tired and thirsty, but there was no water to drink.

"We will not be able to survive without firewood and water!" the men exclaimed sadly. All of them lay down to rest except the merchant.

"I cannot afford to take rest in this hour of crisis! I must find water or all of us shall die!" the merchant thought. "I must find water! I shall not give up!"

He started walking and soon spotted a clump of grass in the desert.

"If there is grass here, there must be water beneath," the merchant concluded and ran back to his men.

"Fetch the spade and the hammer," he shouted. The merchant led his men to the spot and they started digging furiously. After digging for a long time, their spades hit a rock. The men were too tired to dig any further.

"There is water flowing underneath," the merchant exclaimed as he put his ear against the rock. "I can hear it! Don't give up now! Only the strong-willed can achieve something in life. Keep digging, otherwise we all shall die!"

The men started digging again and soon water came gushing out from beneath the broken rock. The merchant and his men shouted with joy. The thirsty men drank this water. After drinking and bathing, the men took out the extra wooden yokes and axles, and used these as firewood. A fire was made and food was cooked. After their meal, the men rested for a while, and resumed their journey. The merchant planted a flag near the watering hole, so that other travellers could see it.

Next morning, the men reached the town, where they sold their goods and made a huge profit. Happy and satisfied, the merchant and his men returned to their village.

The Tricky Wolf
And The Rats
Om
KIDZ
An imprint of Om Books International

Once, a hungry wolf was hunting for food in the forest. Suddenly, he spotted a troop of rats marching towards him. They were led by a huge bandicoot, who was the king of the rats.

"Ah! There's my lunch!" the wolf exclaimed and quickly hid behind a tree so that the rats wouldn't see him. Unaware of his intention, the rats marched straight past the tree behind which the wolf was hiding.

"Hmmm! If I catch one rat and eat him, I shall be full for now but the rest of them would escape and be on their guard," the wolf thought. "There are so many rats! I must think of a way to trick them all so that I shall not run out of food for months."

The wolf decided to follow the rats and reached their hole. Led by the bandicoot, the rats trooped into the hole. When the last rat had entered the hole, the wolf came out of hiding. He had hit upon a brilliant plan to trick the rats!

The wolf stood outside the rat-hole on one leg, with his mouth open and stared at the sun. He waited patiently in this awkward posture till the rats trooped out of their hole once again. They were surprised to see the wolf.

"Why are you standing like this?" the bandicoot asked him.

"If I stood on all my four feet, the Earth would collapse!" the wolf replied.

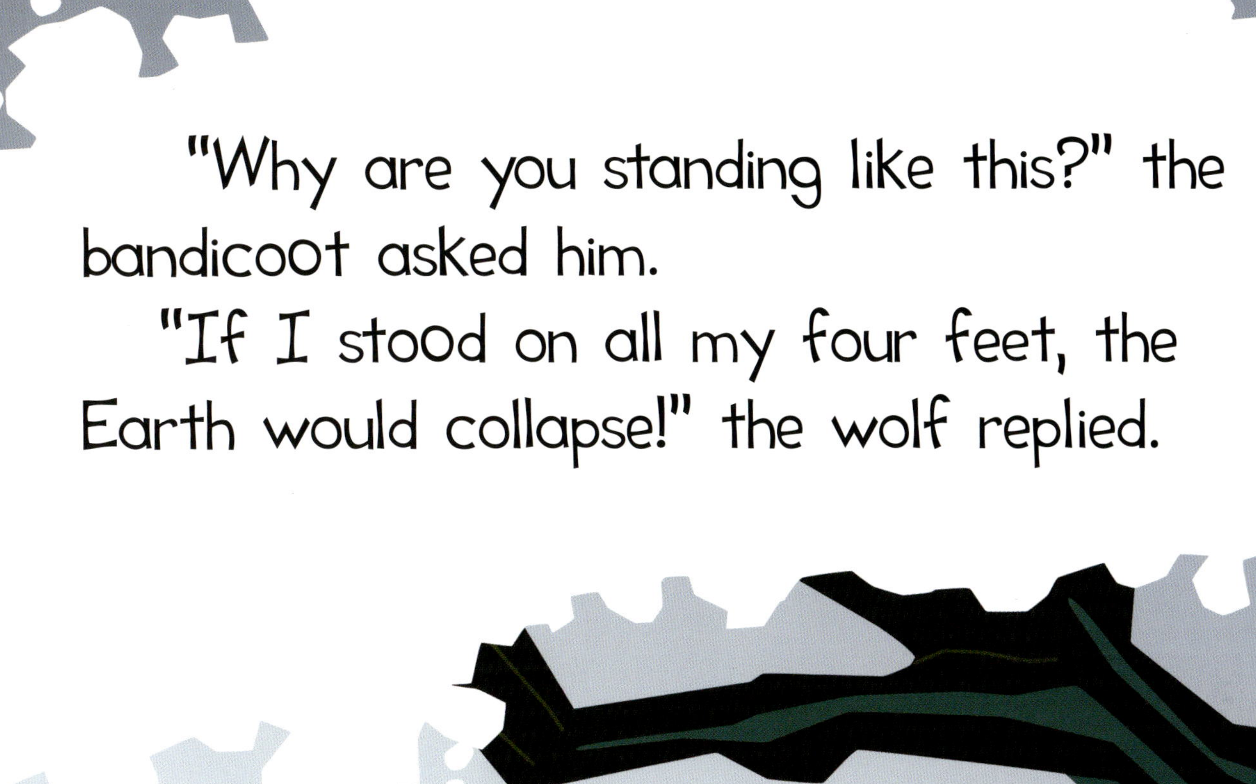

"But why is your mouth open?" the suspicious bandicoot asked.

"I live on air, which is my only food," the wolf replied.

"Why are you staring at the sky?" the king of the rats asked.

"I worship the Almighty Sun God," the wolf replied.

"We are so lucky!" the bandicoot exclaimed. "We have a saint in our midst!"

"We shall pray to this saint every morning and every evening," the bandicoot declared.

The wolf hobbled away happily on one leg, thinking, "The fools actually believed me. My plan is working!"

After that, the rats started worshipping the wolf. As soon as they had finished worshipping the wolf, they turned and marched back into their hole in a single file. The wolf picked up the last rat that was about to enter the hole and had a hearty meal. This continued for many days. But soon, the bandicoot suspected that something was wrong. His suspicion was confirmed when his minister informed him that many rats were missing.

"That saint looks rather healthy for someone who survives only on air," the bandicoot said. "He appears to grow healthier as my subjects go missing. Is he responsible? Well, we shall find out!" he said to his minister.

That evening, as the rats emerged from their hole to pray to the wolf, the bandicoot moved to the end of the line instead of leading his army. After their prayers, the rats turned and marched towards their hole. The wolf jumped on the last rat to catch him! But the bandicoot was ready! He stepped aside and the wolf missed him and fell on the ground. "You shall be punished for killing my subjects, you villain," the bandicoot exclaimed as he jumped on the wolf.

"Attack the wicked wolf!" the minister ordered the rats, who jumped on the wolf and pinned him down. "You have played your trick for the last time, you wicked wolf," the bandicoot cried as he bit the wolf's throat and killed him. After that, the rats made a merry feast.

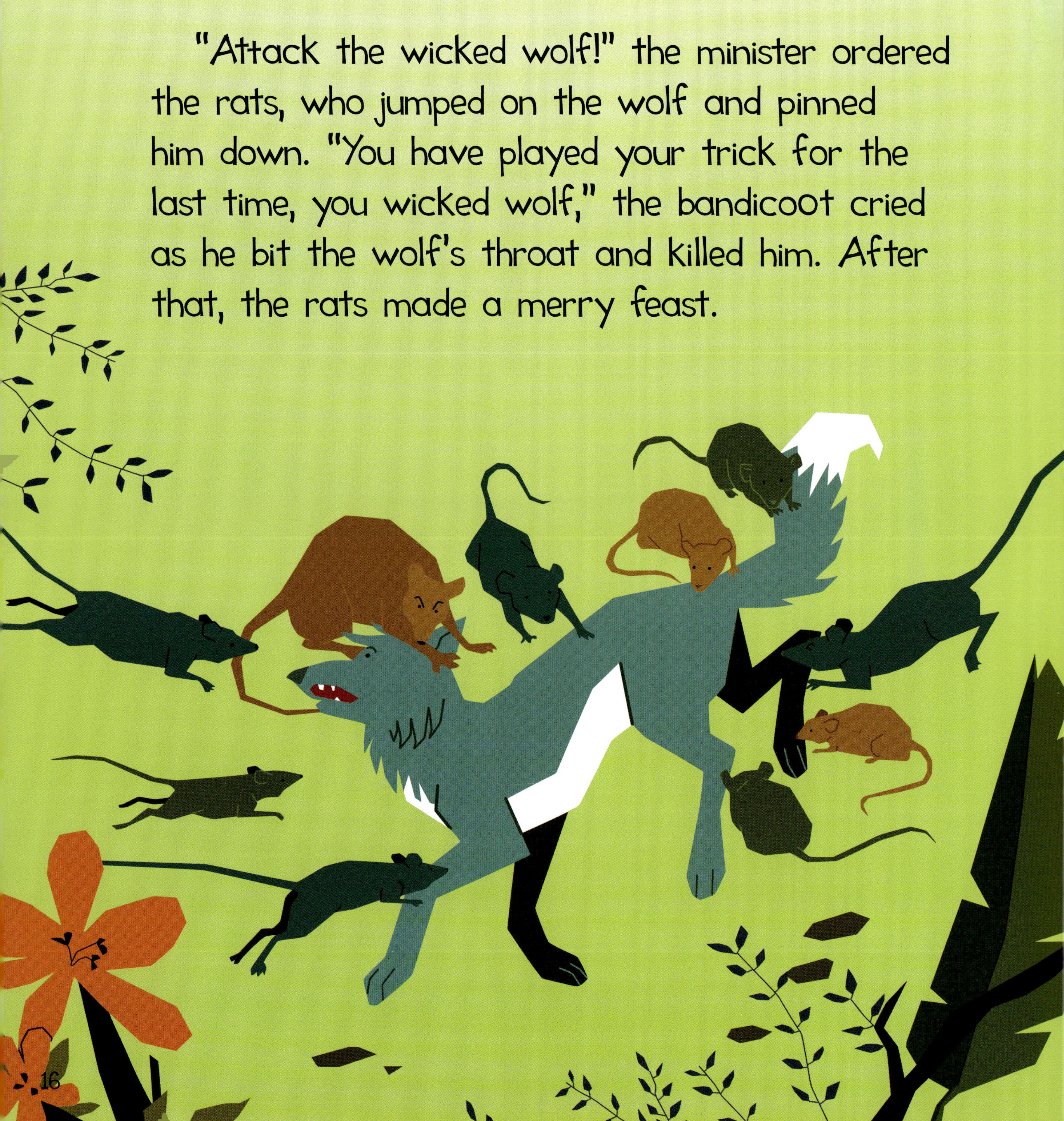